Contents

15 Rules to be a Huge Success in an All-Girl Band

Rule No.

Do you want to be in a successful girl band like All Saints?

15 Rules to be a Huge Success in an All-Girl Band

Girl bands come and go.

When fashions change,
the public lose interest.
The record companies lose interest.

But All Saints are different.

They are a real band,
not just some hopefuls
put together by a record company
to play pop for the kids.

As All Saints put it:
'We're more good-looking than the rest.
And we're more clever!'

All Saints are more streetwise.
And their music speaks for itself.

So, follow their example.
Follow the 15 simples rules
set out in this book.

If you want to be as big as the All Saints,
here's how to do it!

Rule No. 1: Be Gorgeous!

It helps if you're good-looking.

Shaznay, Melanie, Natalie and Nicole
are all drop-dead gorgeous.
In each and every photo.

Of course,
the music is good.
The songs are strong,
and All Saints can really sing.

But with looks likes these,
they have a head start.

Shaznay, Melanie, Natalie and Nicole – all gorgeous. Rule
No. 1 is be gorgeous!

Rule No. 2: Get a Good Education!

If you want a good start in life,
it helps to have a good education.

For three of the All Saints,
Melanie, Natalie and Nicole,
that meant the Sylvia Young Stage School.

Melanie and Nicole started there in 1986.
They have been best friends
from the age of 11.

The Sylvia Young Stage School is famous
for teaching the stars of the future.
People like Emma Bunton
and pop singer Billie,
Nick Berry and Daniella Westbrook
(she played Sam Butcher in EastEnders),
Samantha Janus and Denise Van Outen
all went there.

In fact, the three All Saints
were only in the school for a short time.

Emma Bunton went to the Sylvia Young Stage School.

When Melanie Blatt was young,
doctors discovered that she had a bad back.
She had to have an operation.

Mel's mum is French.
She took Mel to France
for the operation.

Melanie stayed in France for a few years.
She soon settled in
and learnt to speak French.
She took on some acting work as well.

But the music scene was no good.

So in the end,
Melanie came back to London.
She went round the music studios,
hoping for her big break.

And then she met Shaznay Lewis.

Meanwhile,
Natalie and Nicole Appleton
went to live in America.

Their mum and dad got divorced.
Their mum's new boyfriend
is American.

So the girls went to live in New York State.

Born in Canada,
growing up in London,
they go on to finish school in the USA!

Natalie came back to London in 1990.
She met a man,
a dancer called Carl.

They were soon married.
They had a baby girl, Rachel.
But it didn't work out.
Carl left soon after.

It was a hard time for Natalie.
She was devastated and depressed.

But she was lucky.
Her mum came back to London
to help look after baby Rachel.

Rule No. 3: Get Lucky!

When Shaznay Lewis was 16
she spent all her time
hanging round in music studios.

She tried really hard
to make contacts
and get work.

She made a lot of cups of tea.
But she was able to sing some backing vocals
on a few singles.
But she really wanted to sing lead vocals!
She really wanted to sing her own songs!

Shaznay met Melanie
when they were both 21.

They met in a studio near Notting Hill
in north London.
It's called All Saints,
the name of the road outside.

Shaznay and Mel started to work as a duo.
They made a single or two,
but they got nowhere.

Then they got lucky.

Melanie bumped into Nicole Appleton,
her best friend from stage school.
Nicole was back in London.

'It was like we'd never been apart,' says Nicole.
'I had never stopped thinking about Mel.
I just knew we'd meet up again!'

Mel asked Nicole:
'Do you want to join All Saints?'

Nicole said: 'YES!'

Then Natalie started hanging around
with the other three.

She's a year or two older than the rest.
Her experience shows.
Pretty soon she joined All Saints too.

Rule No. 4: Work Hard, Go Hungry!

When they were just Mel and Shaznay,
All Saints signed to ZTT Records.

Their first single 'If You Want to Party'
didn't really do anything.

'We didn't know what we wanted to do,'
Mel explains.
'And ZTT didn't really know
what to do with us!'

Now, All Saints are a four-piece.
Their sound is bigger and better than ever.

The girls signed to London Records,
who made stars of Bananarama
back in the 1980s.

All Saints were on their way.
But there was still some hard work to do.

They had to work in shops
and sell hot dogs
to make ends meet.

Rule No. 5: Be Different!

All Saints want to be different.
It's no good being the same
as every other girl band.

'We're not into Girl Power,'
said Shaznay,
when Girl Power was really big.
'We're into People Power!
No matter who you are,
no matter what sex you are,
Just Go For It!'

They never want to sell out
to the big companies.
They turned down a big deal with Pepsi,
worth half a million pounds.

'I love making music,' Shaznay explains.
'I have no desire to spend the day
doing an advert for cola!'

'We just want our music
to speak for itself,' Nicole adds.

Rule No. 6: Don't Be a Spice Girl!

All Saints made a great demo tape.
It's full of strong songs,
ready to hit the charts.
Lots of top record labels wanted to sign them.
Why did they sign with London Records?

Shaznay explains:
'They were the only ones
who didn't want to turn us into the Spice Girls!'

Mel is more outspoken:
'The day the Spice Girls call themselves artists
I'll kill myself!'

'Don't get me wrong,' she goes on.
'The Spice Girls are good at what they do.
Good luck to them.
It's just that we want to do our own thing.
We don't want to be compared all the time.'

One paper tried to give the All Saints names,
just like the Spice Girls:
Shy Saint, Mouthy Saint.
It didn't catch on.

Rule No. 7: Write Good Songs!

All Saints first single 'I Know Where It's At'
got to No. 4 in the UK charts.

'Never Ever', the second single,
is a slow sexy song.
Sad and bluesy.
Shaznay wrote it four years before,
after she broke up with someone.

'Never Ever' took nine weeks to get to No. 1.

But it sold 770,000 copies
on the way to the top spot.
That's more than any other single
in chart history.

It's a mega-hit in 15 countries
around the world.

The next two singles
went straight to No. 1 as well.
In all, there are five singles
on the All Saints' first album.
The album came out in 1997
and sold over 600,000 copies by January 1998.

Later, Shaznay writes a song
for the cult movie *The Beach*.
The song is called 'Pure Shores',
and went straight to No. 1 in March 2000.

All Saints worked hard to get where they are today. They spend a lot of time doing concerts.

Rule No. 8: Win a Few Awards!

In February 1998,
All Saints had tears in their eyes.
They won two Brit Awards.

'Never Ever' was Best Single
and Best Video.

The same year,
they also have a shot at Best Newcomer
in the MoBO Awards.
MoBO stands for Music of Black Origin.

And late in 1999,
Natalie won a Style Award
from *Elle* magazine.
She's 'Most Stylish Couple',
along with her new man,
Trainspotting star Jonny Lee Miller.

In 2000, they won the Best Pop Act Award
at the MTV Europe Music Awards.

All Saints performed at the MoBO Awards, but didn't win an award.

Rule No. 9: Play Sell-Out Shows to Famous People!

In February 1998,
All Saints sang 'Never Ever'
at the Brit Awards.

Later that year,
they sang for Tony Blair
at the G8 summit meeting for world leaders.

The Prime Minister is a big All Saints fan!
So is President Clinton.
So is the Sultan of Brunei,
one of the richest men in the world.
He is said to have paid £1 million
for a private All Saints concert!
Prince Charles is a big fan too.

In July 1998,
All Saints sang at the Prince's Trust Concert.
It was the biggest concert in
London for over 20 years.
(When All Saints came on,
Prince Charles grabbed a pair of binoculars
for a better look!)

Rule No. 10: Wear the Right Clothes!

When CATs and cargo pants are in fashion,
All Saints wear CATs and cargo pants.

When DKNY is the only label to wear,
All Saints wear DKNY.

They don't put on special clothes
when they go on stage.
They just wear what's comfy.

'I just wear what I always used to wear,'
says Mel.
'I wear the same when I go to the supermarket!'

Even so, All Saints are always out there,
at the front of fashion,
in Calvin Klein or Nike,
in Tommy Hilfiger or Diesel,
in Levis or Air Max sneakers.

In fact, Melanie says
that the best bit about being famous is . . .
the free sneakers!

Rule No. 10 is wear the right clothes! All Saints are always ahead of fashion.

Rule No. 11: Campaign!

It helps if you stand up
for what you believe in.

If All Saints see a good cause,
they join the campaign.

In 1998,
they sang for the Prince's Trust,
a charity working with young people.

In 1999, they campaigned against hunting,
and against land-mines,
which kill and maim people all over the world.

And there's an All Saints song
(called 'Trapped')
on an album called 'Wicked Women'.
It was sold to make money
to fight breast cancer.

All Saints stand up for things they believe in. In 1998 they
sang at the Prince's Trust charity concert.

Rule No. 12: Date the Right People!

It helps if you date famous people.
And it helps if they are as good-looking as you!
(See Rule No. 1!)

Best of all are film stars
or other pop people.

Natalie dated TV presenter
Jamie Theakston
for nearly a year.

Then she heard that he'd been seeing someone else.

Nat smacked him in the face,
and finished with him.
'I just don't trust him any more,' she says.

Then she went out with Jonny Lee Miller.

'This is the real deal!' she told the press.
'I didn't know what love was.
Until now.'

But in January 2000,
Natalie and Jonny split up.
She was heart-broken.

'Will we stay friends?' she asks.
'Will we get back together?
Who knows?'

Rule No. 12 is date the right people! Natalie was
heartbroken when she split up with Johnny Lee Miller.

Nicole had the same feelings
for Robbie Williams.
But they split up
seven weeks after they got engaged.

'It took a long time to break up,'
she tells us.
'About a year.
But I'm over it now.
Ten years from now, maybe,
Robbie and I will be able to laugh about it.
But not yet.'

But when Nicole asks herself:
'What are the good things
about being single?'
the answer is:
'I don't think there are any!'

In 2000 she is dating Liam Gallagher
who left Patsy to be with her…

When All Saints were working on 'The Beach',
there was some gossip.
About Shaznay and Leo di Caprio!

'That just made me howl with laughter!'
she says now.

The reason?
Shaznay is already happy,
and in love.
Her boyfriend is a dancer called Christian.

Melanie is happy, and in love, too.
Stuart Zender is a bass player.
He used to be in Jamiroquai.

Lily Ella was born
on November 2nd 1998.
Now Stuart is a full-time father
looking after his new baby daughter.

The Lily part of her name
is from the flowers that Stuart gave to Mel.
The Ella part of her name
is from Mel's favourite jazz singer,
Ella Fitzgerald.

Melanie had to take a break
from All Saints work
when Lily Ella was born.

In November 2000,
Nicole tells everyone she is pregnant.
People start to wonder if Nicole
and Liam will get married.

Rule No. 13: Don't Work Too Hard!

In 1998, All Saints were working too hard.
The press was too much,
and all four women felt it.

Melanie was still touring,
all over the world,
just weeks before Lily Ella was due.

In December 1998, Nicole and Shaznay
had a fall-out.
The trouble was,
it was live on MTV.

There was talk of an All Saints split.
Nicole went missing.
Melanie was having a baby.
Shaz and Natalie held it all together.
The two of them went to America.
They managed to keep up appearances.

In the end,
Nicole stayed with the band.
It was manager John Benson
who had to go.
He had a £1 million pay-off
in February 1999.

Rule No. 14: Make a Movie!

Before the All Saints' second album came out,
Melanie, Natalie and Nicole
starred in a movie.

It was made by Dave Stewart,
from the Eurythmics.

The movie's called *Honest*.

'We just get to play ourselves,' says Nicole.
'Nat plays the wild one.
Mel is the quiet one.
and I'm in between.
Just like we are in real life!'

Honest is set in the 1960s.
It's about three girls
who dress as men
in order to go and rob banks.

But the movie is most famous
for when the girls are *undressed*!

Nicole and Natalie appear
in one or two nude scenes.

'I was a bit shy at first,' says Natalie,
'but only about showing my mum and dad!
We had a copy on video.
I had to fast-forward the rude bits!'

Rule No. 15: Break and Make Up!

In January 2001,
the band have a big bust-up – again!

As always there are rumours about
the reason for the split.
Some think there was an argument over a jacket.

But the problems go much deeper.
Tours are cancelled, money is lost.
The All Saints all start to look for solo careers.

It may not be for real.
It may be good for publicity
– to split up and get back together.
Keep everyone guessing.

But the fans are gutted. And confused.

After all, the All Saints were riding high in the charts,
singing happily:

'I wouldn't want to be anywhere else but here!
I wouldn't want to change!'

What happened to the best girl band in the world?